The Answers You Seek

Are Within

Divine Messengers

Angelic Words of Strength & Support

Amanda M Clarke

Koru Lifestylist

KORU (Maori:NZ)
A symbol of spiritual growth and spiritual connection.

Copyright © Amanda M Clarke 2025
KORU Publishing

All rights reserved. All content, materials, and intellectual property in this book or any other platform owned by Koru Publishing are protected by copyright laws. This includes text, images, graphics, videos, audio, software, and any other form of content that may be produced by Koru Publishing.

No part of this content may be reproduced, distributed, or transmitted in any form or by any means without the prior written permission of Koru Publishing. This means that you cannot copy, reproduce, or use any of the content in this book for commercial or personal purposes without the express written consent of Koru Publishing.

Unauthorized use of any copyrighted material owned by Koru Publishing may result in legal action being taken against you. Koru Publishing reserves the right to pursue all available legal remedies against any individual or entity found to be infringing on its copyright.

In summary, Koru Publishing © 2024 holds exclusive rights to all the content produced by it, and any unauthorized use of such content will result in legal action.

KORU Publishing

KORU (Maori:NZ)
A symbol of spiritual growth and spiritual connection.

Rocky Point Townhouse, CHRISTMAS ISLAND, Western Australia 6798

ISBN: 978-1-7637496-9-6

Introduction to Angels

Across cultures and centuries, angels have been seen as messengers of light - divine beings who bridge the realms of heaven and earth. They appear in sacred texts, works of art, and the whispered stories passed down through generations, always carrying the same promise: you are loved, you are guided, and you are never alone.

Angels are not distant or unreachable. They walk beside you in moments of joy, in times of doubt, and during every season of change. They remind you of your own divine spark and encourage you to see the strength, beauty, and wisdom that already dwell within your soul.

This book is an invitation to open your heart and connect with them more deeply. Each page holds a message and a mantra, designed to bring comfort, clarity, and inspiration. Allow these divine messengers to speak to you, and let their light guide your journey.

Disclaimer: Divine Messengers: Angelic Words of Strength & Support is intended for inspirational, spiritual, and entertainment purposes only. The messages and mantras contained within this book reflect intuitive insights and creative interpretations, and are not a substitute for professional medical, psychological, financial, or legal advice.

If you are experiencing physical, emotional, or mental health concerns, please consult with a qualified healthcare professional or licensed counselor. The author and publisher make no representations or warranties regarding the accuracy, applicability, or completeness of the information provided.

By reading this book, you acknowledge that you are responsible for your own choices, actions, and well-being. Neither the author nor the publisher shall be held liable for any loss, damage, or consequences arising directly or indirectly from the use of this material.

Trust your intuition, seek guidance when needed, and use these messages as gentle tools for reflection and inspiration.

How to use this book

STEP ONE: CLEAR YOUR BOOKS ENERGY

Since your book is a sensitive instrument and has been through many hands to reach you, you will need to clear it of any energy it may have absorbed. Steps One and Two only need to be completed every so often when the energies of the book become clogged.

It is a good idea to ground yourself first before clearing the book. Do this by sitting on a standard kitchen chair, with your feet comfortably flat on the floor. You can do this with shoes on, but it is better in bare feet. Better still, stand barefoot on the ground in the open, this will ensure all energies will be fully grounded out into the nothingness of the earth.

Hold the book in the palm of your non dominant hand as this is the hand that receives energy.

Form a fist with your other hand and knock on the book once with your fist sending all energies from the book to the ground and into nothingness.

This clears out the old energy and the book is now blank and is ready to be imbued with your energy.

STEP TWO: CONSECRATE THE BOOK

Flip through the pages of the book ensuring you touch every page with your thumb, fingers or hand. This will start infusing it with your energy.

Hold the book in your dominant hand up to your heart and think about the prayers or intentions you would like to infuse the book with. For example, you may say to yourself in your minds eye or aloud:

'I ask that all of my readings with this book be accurate and specific, and bring blessings to everyone involved. Please help me stay centred in my higher self so that I may hear, see, feel, and know the messages that wish to come through these readings'

You may wish to keep your book wrapped in a silk scarf or unique bag as this will keep other people's energies from transferring to your pages.

STEP THREE: INVOKE THE ARCHANGELS

a. Find yourself a safe and comfortable place, somewhere quiet and you feel at peace.

b. Take 3 deep breaths to clear the mind. Inhale deeply through your nose, exhale through your lips and close your eyes.

c. Ask the Archangels to be present around you. Visualise a bright white orb of light surrounding you. Ask out aloud or in your minds eye:

'Archangels, I ask that you stay by my side and watch over me during this reading, ensuring that only Gods love and wisdom come through. I trust that you will guide me toward the best outcome. Thank you for your presence and guidance'

STEP FOUR: ASK A QUESTION

Think of a question you would like that answer to. If you're giving a reading for someone else, ask him or her to either think of or verbalize a question. The archangels hear your thoughts, so you need not voice your queries aloud.

STEP FIVE: CHOOSE A PAGE

Take a deep breath and open your eyes.
Flip through the book. You may flip backward and forward using your thumbs or any method you choose. You may just open the book to a page, or keep flipping through the pages until you feel the sense to stop. You may even hear in your thoughts 'Stop,' or a page may just grab.

STEP SIX: THE ARCHANGELS MESSAGE

Read the passage on the archangel and the message they wish to convey to you. Take a moment and reflect on the message. Pay attention to any thoughts or feelings that come to you, as they are a part of the answer. Each Archangel comes with a 'Mantra' which you can say aloud or to yourself, calling upon the archangel to guide you.

Dedication

For every soul who has ever searched for a sign,
for those who have whispered prayers in the stillness of the night,
and for the dreamers who dare to believe in unseen wings.
May these pages remind you that you are never walking alone.
May they guide you back to the light when shadows fall.
And may the words of the angels awaken in you the strength,
the courage, and the love that have always been yours.

With deepest gratitude and love,

- Amanda M Clarke

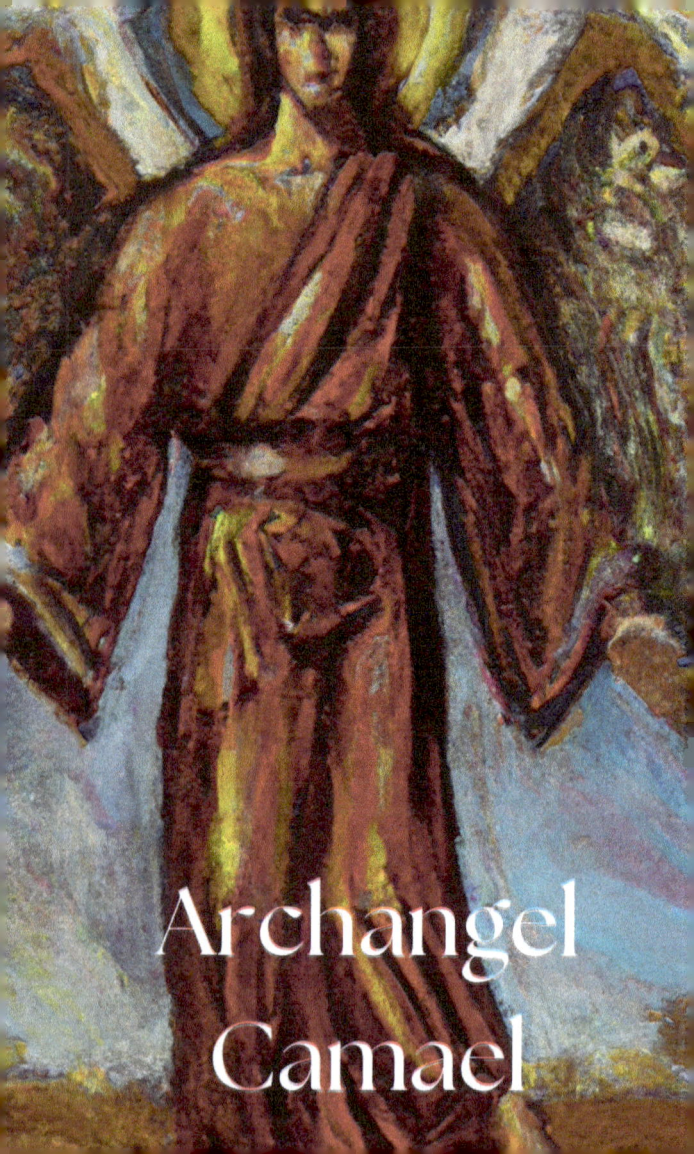

I am Camael, and I bring you strength and courage. Whatever obstacle stands before you, know this: you have the power to rise above it. Within you is a well of resilience deeper than you imagine. Trust in your abilities, trust in your heart, and take each step with faith.

You are never alone in your struggles. Call upon me and the angels, and we will surround you with guidance, protection, and support. Stand tall in your truth. Speak with conviction, even when doubt or opposition presses against you.

I encourage you to follow your intuition and honor the voice within. When you choose courage over fear and conviction over silence, you step into your true power. Stand firm, believe in your strength, and know I am by your side as you face all that comes.

Archangel Camael Mantra...

I call upon Archangel Camael to fill me with strength and courage. I trust my inner power and stand tall in my truth.

I am Jophiel, and I bring the gift of beauty, creativity, and inspiration. Look around you now - notice the colors of nature, the light in another's smile, the quiet details that often go unseen. When you honor beauty in your world, you awaken gratitude and joy within your soul.

I urge you to express your own creativity, in whatever form your heart desires - through art, music, writing, or simply the way you live each day. In creating, you uncover your wisdom and connect with your highest self.

Do not forget to seek inspiration from the divine. In prayer, in meditation, or in stillness, I will guide you back to the light. Beauty surrounds you always. Let it inspire you, lift you, and remind you of your true radiance.

Archangel Jophiel Mantra...

I call upon Archangel Jophiel to open my eyes to beauty and fill my heart with inspiration. I create with joy, and I shine with gratitude

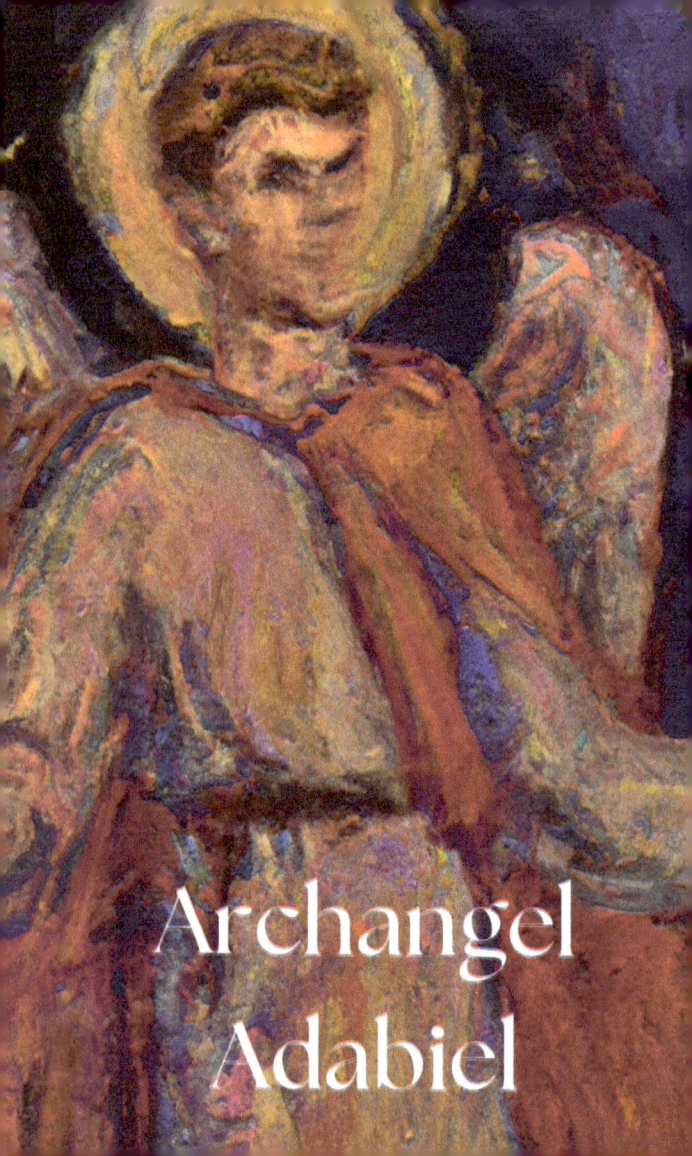

Archangel Adabiel's divine message is one of hope and inspiration. Adabiel reminds us that we are capable of achieving our dreams and that we have the power within us to make them a reality. The angel encourages us to believe in ourselves and to trust that the universe will support us on our journey.

Adabiel also reminds us that every challenge we face is an opportunity for growth and learning. The angel encourages us to embrace these challenges and to use them as stepping stones towards our goals.

Overall, Archangel Adabiel's message is one of empowerment and encouragement. The angel reminds us that we are not alone on our journey and that we have the support of the universe behind us. By believing in ourselves and staying focused on our goals, we can achieve anything we set our minds to.

Archangel Adabiel Mantra...

"I ask you Adabiel to give me hope and inspiration to support me in acheiving my dreams.' I believe in me"

I am Azrael, the angel of comfort and transformation. I walk beside you in the moments when life feels heavy, when grief presses against your heart, when endings leave you feeling empty. I remind you that death is not an ending but a doorway - a passage into greater light. Those you love who have crossed over are not lost to you; they continue to surround you with love, whispering guidance, and watching over your path.

Change can be difficult, and at times it may feel as though the ground beneath you has shifted beyond recognition. Yet within every ending lies a beginning, and within every loss, a seed of new life is waiting to grow. Trust that the universe is guiding you into a new chapter filled with hope. Release what no longer serves you. Embrace transformation with courage, and know that you are never walking alone.

Archangel Azrael Mantra...

"I call upon Archangel Azrael to wrap me in peace and comfort. I release what I cannot hold. I welcome transformation, and I trust that love never dies."

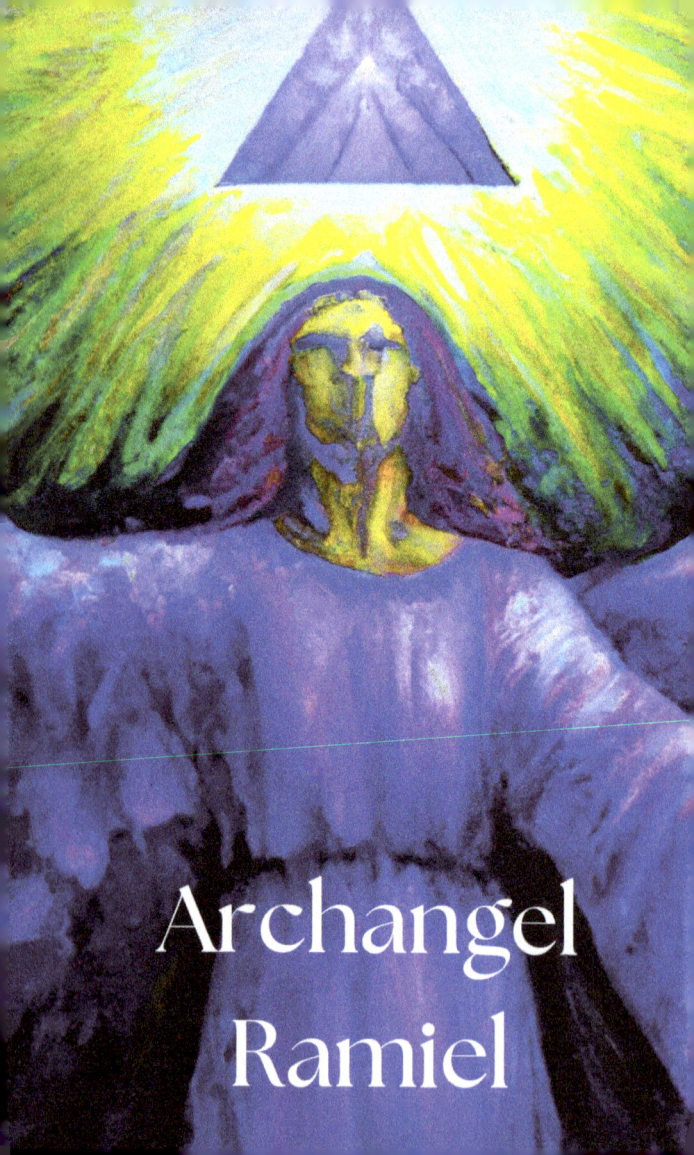

I am Ramiel, angel of hope and renewal. I come to remind you that even in your darkest hour, a sacred flame still burns within you. No shadow, no trial, and no mistake can extinguish the light of your soul. When the weight of the past presses on your heart, lift your eyes and remember: you are stronger than you know, and you are never without support.

I encourage you to trust in yourself, to believe that your dreams are not only possible but destined to bloom when you take bold steps forward. Release the heaviness of old wounds and forgive - forgive others, and just as importantly, forgive yourself. In forgiveness you will find freedom, and in freedom, the path ahead will become clear.

You are a powerful creator of your life. With courage, faith, and my guidance, you can bring your deepest visions into reality.

Archangel Ramiel Mantra...

"I call upon Archangel Ramiel to renew my spirit with hope. I release the past, embrace forgiveness, and step boldly into the life my soul is ready to create."

I am Jerahmeel, angel of hope and encouragement. I come to remind you that even in your darkest hour, a spark of light is always present. No shadow, no challenge, no sorrow can extinguish the divine flame within you. Hold fast to hope, for it is the bridge that carries you from despair into renewal.

I invite you to open your heart to new opportunities and possibilities. Life is forever offering fresh paths, yet they may require you to step beyond the familiar and take bold risks. Do not fear this. Within you lies untapped strength and gifts waiting to be awakened. When you dare to move forward, you will discover how capable and radiant you truly are.

Above all, treat yourself and others with compassion. Love, forgiveness, and kindness are your greatest powers. Walk in hope, stand in faith, and shine your light wherever you go.

Archangel Jerahmeel Mantra...

"I call upon Archangel Jerahmeel to fill my heart with hope and courage. I welcome new opportunities, release fear, and embrace love and compassion on my path."

I am Muriel, angel of peace and compassion, and I come to surround you with my gentle presence. I see the weight you have carried, the moments of stress and worry that have pressed against your heart. I remind you now to pause, to breathe, and to honor your need for rest. Self-care is not selfish - it is sacred. When you nurture your own soul, you create space for healing and for love to flow freely again.

Allow yourself to be held in my light. Release the heaviness, the doubts, and the emotions that no longer serve you. Let them dissolve in my embrace, so that peace may take their place. Know that you are cherished, guided, and never alone.

You are worthy of compassion. You are worthy of love. Trust that balance will return, and that I walk beside you, bringing harmony to your heart and life.

Archangel Muriel Mantra...

"I call upon Archangel Muriel to surround me with peace and compassion. I release all heaviness and open my heart to love, balance, and divine harmony."

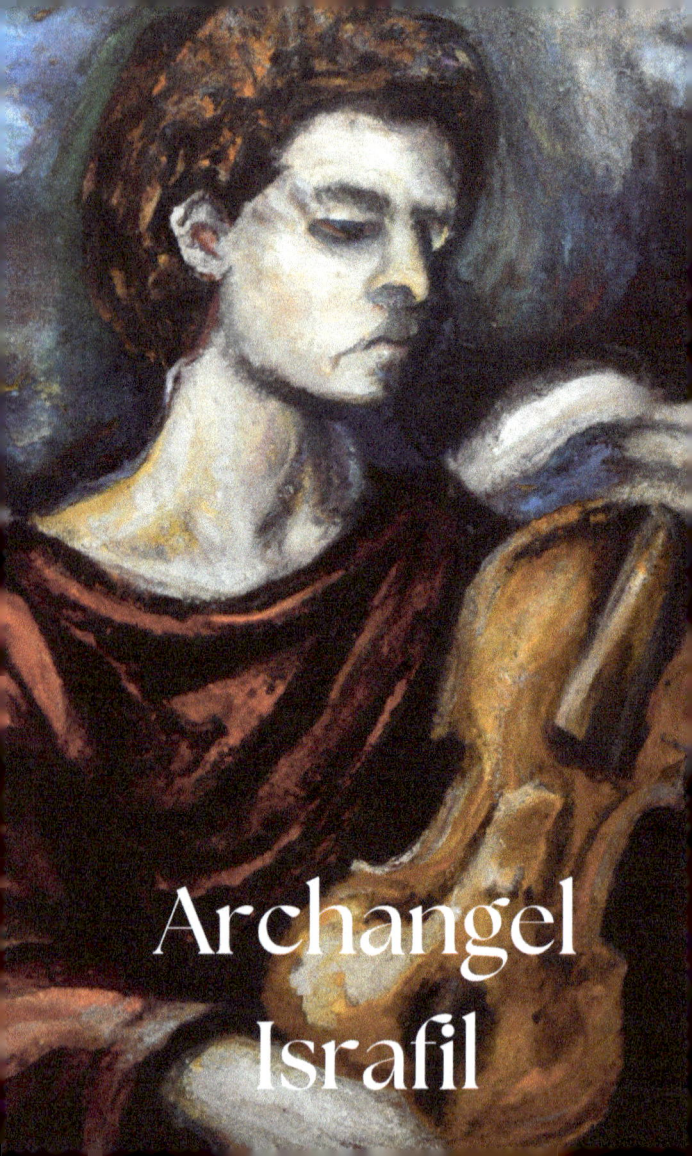

I am Israfil, the angel of harmony and sacred sound. I remind you that all of creation is a divine symphony, and you are an irreplaceable note within it. Your presence carries a frequency that no other soul can replicate, and when you allow your true self to shine, the universe sings in balance.

Open your heart to the music that surrounds you - the rhythm of your breath, the song of the wind, the pulse of life moving through every moment. Sound is the language of the cosmos, a bridge between the seen and unseen, and through it you can hear the voice of the Divine.

Even when life feels chaotic or uncertain, trust in the greater harmony being woven through your days. Every step, every pause, every note has its place. Align with this sacred order, and you will discover peace, purpose, and unity with all that is.

Archangel Israphil Mantra...

"I call upon Archangel Israfil to fill my spirit with harmony and song. I open my heart to divine rhythm, trusting that every note of my life plays its perfect part."

I am Raphael, the healer of God's light, and I come to you with hands outstretched, ready to guide you into wholeness. My love for you is vast and unconditional – it surrounds you, upholds you, and reminds you that you are never alone on your journey.

Healing is not only the mending of the body. It is the gentle restoration of your mind, the soothing of your emotions, and the awakening of your spirit. Wherever you feel burdened, weary, or uncertain, invite me in. Allow me to help you release the pain, fear, or beliefs that no longer serve your highest truth.

You are a radiant soul, filled with divine light and infinite potential. Trust in the sacred flow of the universe, for every experience is guiding you toward balance, peace, and joy. Call upon me, and together we will heal, restore, and lift you into wholeness.

Archangel Raphael Mantra...

"I call upon Archangel Raphael to surround me with healing light. I release all pain and fear, and I open myself to wholeness, peace, and divine love."

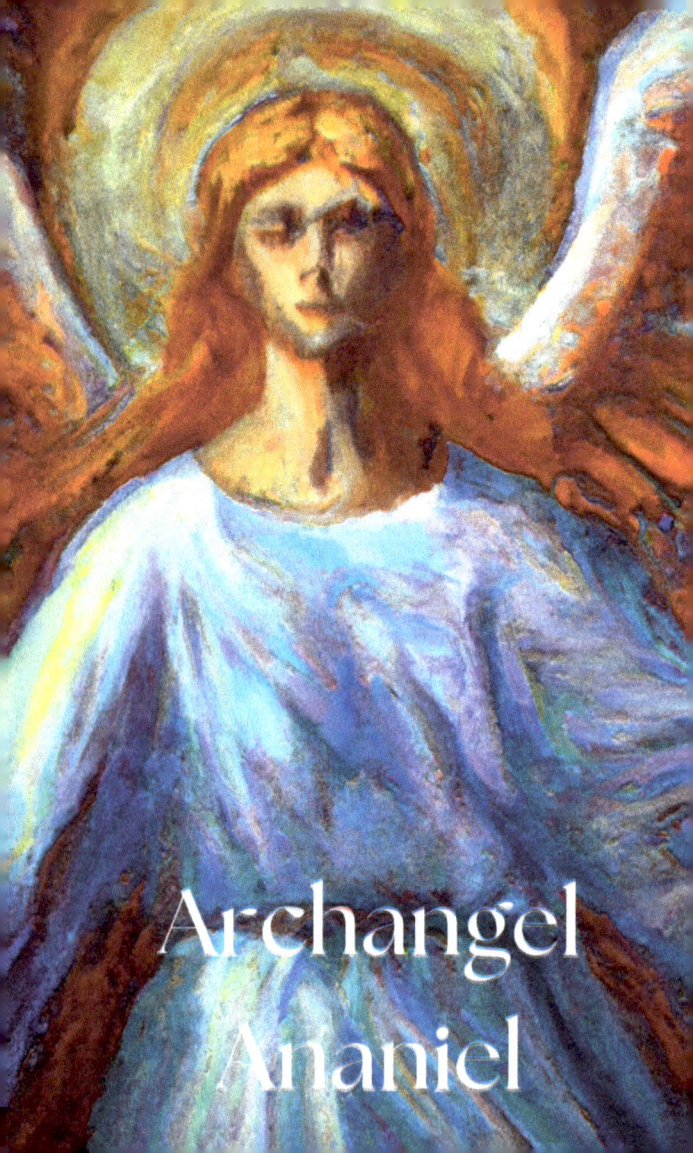

I am Ananiel, angel of awakening and spiritual growth. I come to guide you deeper into the truth of who you are. Within you lives a higher self - radiant, eternal, and wise - and it longs for your attention. Take time to pause, to breathe, to turn inward. In stillness, in meditation, and in prayer, you will hear the whispers of your soul and the voice of the Divine calling you forward.

I remind you that you are never alone on this journey. Even in moments of doubt or silence, I am beside you, and the universe surrounds you with love and guidance. Trust that every experience, whether joyful or challenging, is shaping you into the person you are meant to become.

Open yourself to discovery. Honor the sacred unfolding within you. Walk with faith, and I will light your path as you grow in spirit and truth.

Archangel Ananiel Mantra...

"I call upon Archangel Ananiel to guide me on my path of awakening. I trust the wisdom of my soul and open my heart to divine growth and discovery."

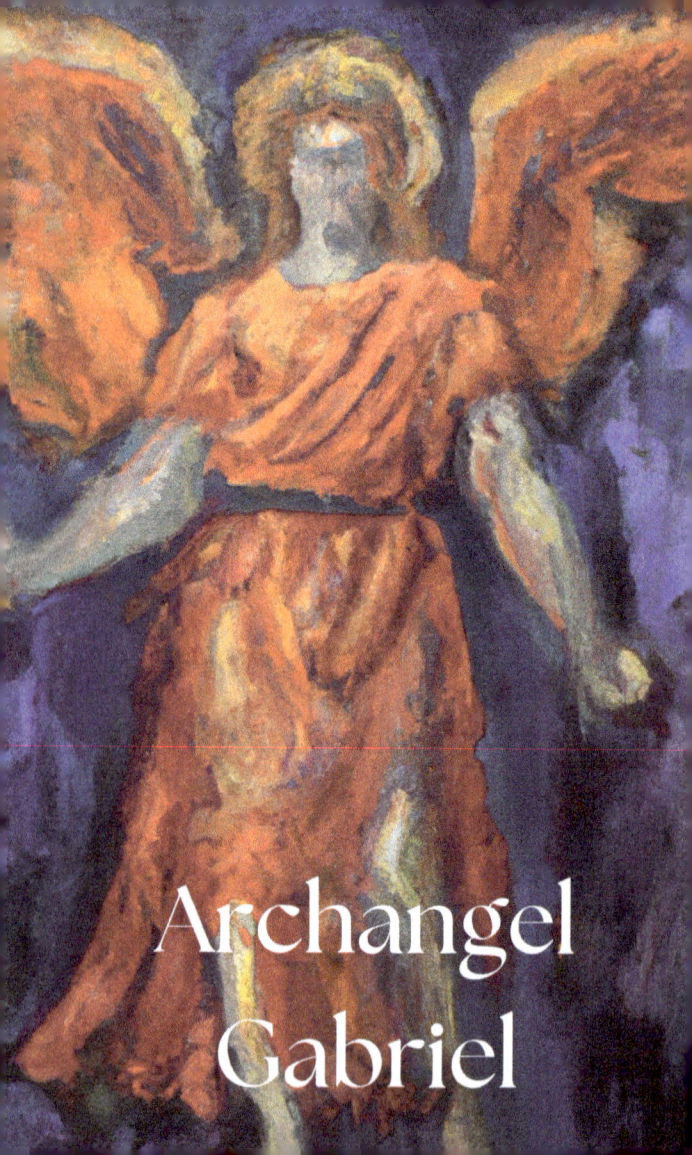

I am Gabriel, messenger of light, and I come to remind you of the gift within your voice and the power of your creativity. You carry ideas, visions, and expressions that are meant to be shared, for they hold the ability to uplift, inspire, and guide others. Do not hide your light. Speak with clarity and with love, for your words are instruments of healing and truth.

In your relationships, in your work, in the quiet moments of self expression, choose to communicate openly and with compassion. Listen deeply to others, for connection flows in both directions. I encourage you to trust your creativity, trust your voice, and allow them to shape the world around you. Your words and actions ripple outward, carrying influence and inspiration. Use them well, and you will awaken beauty and light wherever you go.

.

Archangel Gabriel Mantra...

'I call upon Archangel Gabriel to awaken my voice and creativity. I speak with clarity, love, and truth. My words inspire, my actions uplift, and my heart listens with compassion.'

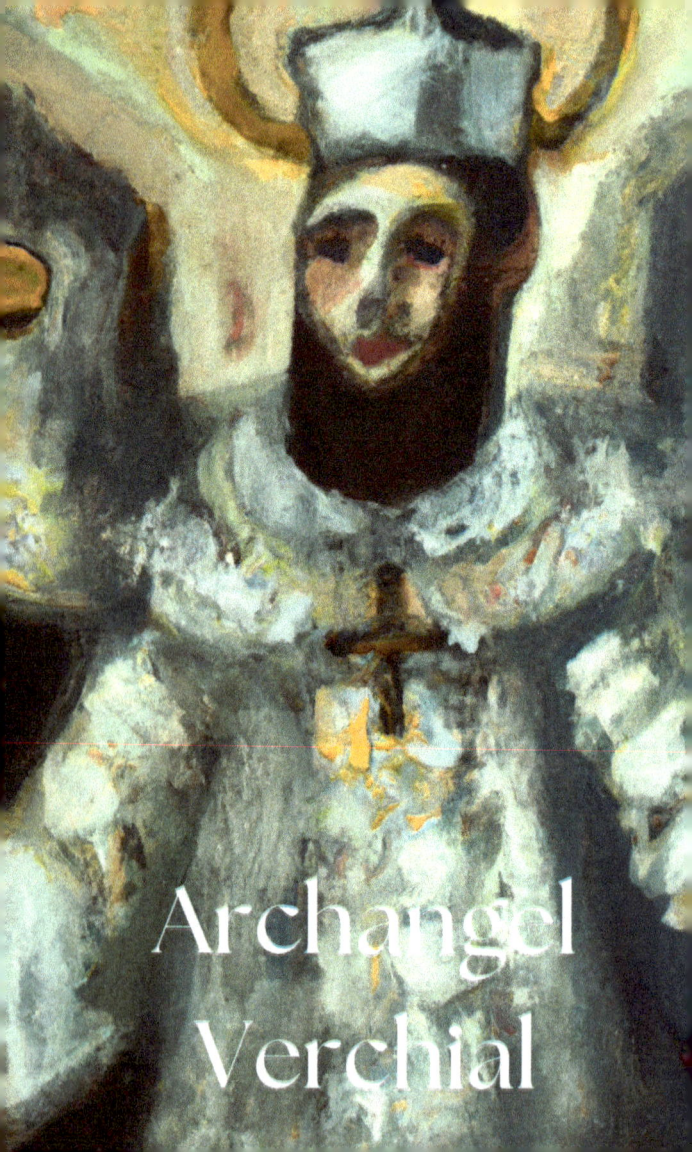

I am Verchial, angel of abundance and divine prosperity. I come to remind you that you are not separate from the flow of creation - you are a co creator of your reality. Within you lies the power to shape your life, to dream boldly, and to bring those dreams into form. Trust the universe, for it longs to support you and provide what you truly need.

Stay focused on your goals and hold them with faith. Fear and doubt may whisper that you are unworthy or unprepared, but these are illusions. With determination and trust, you can rise above them. Remember always to give thanks for what you already have, for gratitude is the key that opens the door to more blessings.

I invite you to share your abundance with others. As you give, you receive, and as you uplift those around you, your own light grows stronger. Know that you are deeply loved and fully supported.

Archangel Verchial Mantra...

"I call upon Archangel Verchial to awaken the flow of abundance in my life. I trust the universe, give with joy, and gratefully receive the blessings prepared for me."

Archangel Raguel brings a message of harmony and balance. He reminds us that every relationship, whether it be with others or with ourselves, is a sacred and precious bond that should be nurtured with care and respect.

He encourages us to seek out peaceful resolutions to conflicts, to forgive ourselves and others, and to strive for fairness and justice in all our interactions. Through his loving guidance, we can learn to let go of anger, bitterness, and resentment, and instead, cultivate compassion, empathy, and understanding.

Trust in his presence to help bring order and balance to any situation, and to heal any wounds that may have caused discord or disharmony in our lives.

Archangel Raguel Mantra...

"Archangel Raguel, I invite your presence to bring peace and harmony to my relationships and within myself. Help me to let go of any anger or resentment, and to forgive myself and others."

I am Michael, protector and guide, and I stand beside you now with the strength of a thousand suns. Trust in your own power, for it flows from the same divine source that created the stars. You may feel tested, weighed down by fear, doubt, or obstacles that seem impossible to move, but know this: you are stronger than you realize. When the shadows rise, call on me. I will surround you with my shield of light and help you release what no longer serves you.

Believe in yourself, for you are capable of far more than you've been led to believe. The universe is guiding you, placing each step in divine timing. Stay faithful to your path, even when it feels uncertain. With my protection, your courage, and the support of the heavens, there is nothing beyond your reach.

Archangel Michael Mantra...

'Archangel Michael, protect and guide me on my path. Fill me with your strength and courage, and help me release any fears or doubts. I trust in your power to keep me safe and to lead me towards my highest good. Thank you for your love and protection.'

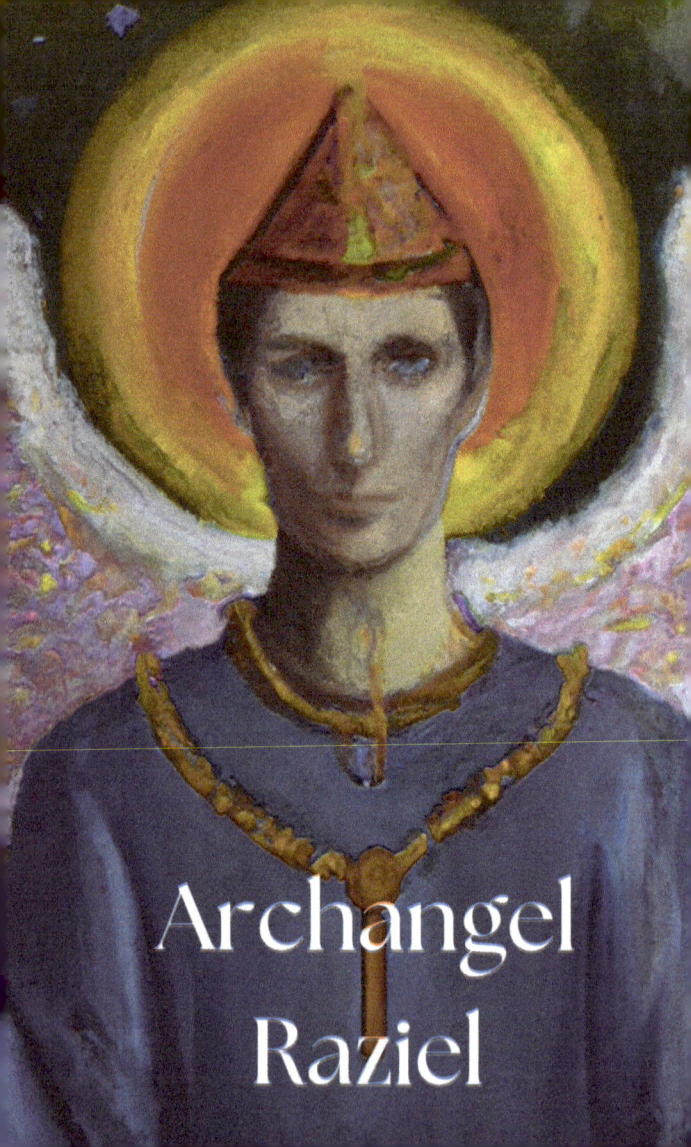

I am Raziel, keeper of divine secrets and hidden wisdom. You are ready now to receive the knowledge the universe has been preparing for you. Pay attention to the signs, the whispers, the patterns unfolding around you - each one is guiding you toward your true purpose.

You are walking the path of awakening, and though at times it may feel overwhelming, trust that every step is for your highest good. I remind you that you are a powerful co creator. Your thoughts, your focus, your intentions are not small things - they shape your reality.

Stay clear in what you truly desire. Hold your vision with faith, and watch as the universe aligns to meet you. Know that you are guided, supported, and never alone in this unfolding journey of light and truth.

Archangel Raziel Mantra...

Archangel Raziel, I call upon your divine wisdom and guidance. Help me connect with the knowledge and insights of the universe'

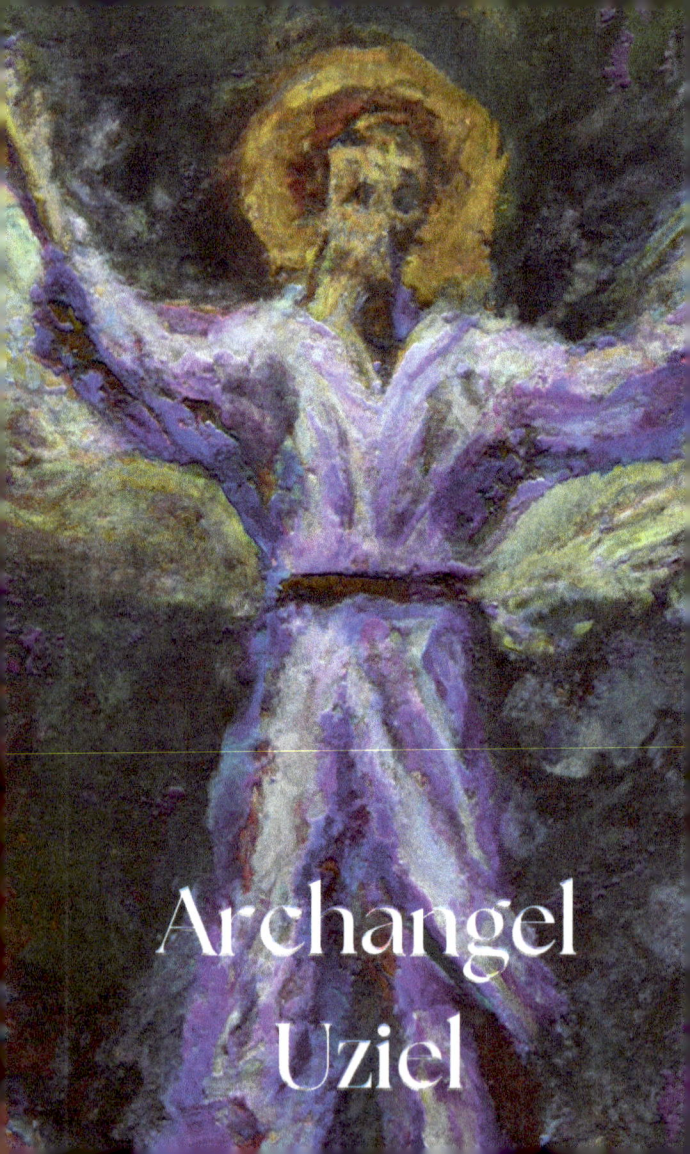

I am Uziel, angel of strength, courage, and perseverance. I come to remind you that within your spirit lives a well of power deeper than you can see. No matter the challenges before you, you carry the wisdom and resilience to overcome them. Do not doubt your ability to rise, for every trial is shaping you into the strong, radiant being you are destined to become.

Stay true to your path, beloved one. The world may offer distractions, opinions, and pressures that seek to turn you away from your purpose, but your heart knows the way. Trust in your inner guidance, and let your soul's quiet voice be louder than the noise around you.

I encourage you to take bold action and step beyond the familiar. Growth awaits outside the walls of comfort. Walk forward with courage, knowing I am with you, guiding, strengthening, and lifting you always.

Archangel Uziel Mantra…

"I call upon Archangel Uziel to fill me with strength and perseverance. I trust my inner wisdom, walk my true path, and move forward with courage."

I am Daniel, angel of strength and courage, and I am here to remind you of the power that dwells within your soul. No obstacle is greater than the light you carry, no challenge too heavy for the spirit that lives inside you. When difficulties rise before you, do not shrink back. Call upon me, and I will stand with you, surrounding you with courage and guiding your steps forward.

I encourage you to remain true to yourself, to walk in the integrity of your values even when the path feels steep or uncertain. The world may press against you, but your voice, your truth, and your resilience are stronger than any resistance. Trust that each trial is shaping you, preparing you, and aligning you with the divine plan.

Stand firm, beloved one, for you are never alone. With faith and courage, you can overcome all things.

Archangel Daniel Mantra...

"I call upon Archangel Daniel to strengthen my heart with courage and faith. I stand firm in my truth and walk forward with trust in the divine plan."

I, Archangel Sachiel, come to bring you a message of hope and abundance. The universe is abundant, and you are a divine being with the power to manifest your desires. Trust in yourself and in the power of the universe to provide for you. Remember to express gratitude for all that you already have and trust that more is on the way.

As you navigate through life's challenges, call upon me for guidance and support. I am here to assist you in finding the courage and strength to overcome any obstacles in your path. Trust that you are never alone, and we angels are always here to guide and support you.

Blessings be upon you.

Archangel Sachiel Mantra...

"Divine Archangel Sachiel, I call upon you now. Please bring to me abundance, prosperity and flow. Clear any blocks or obstacles that I may face. And guide me towards opportunities that lead to grace. Thank you for your loving presence and support. I am open to receive all that you may report. With gratitude and trust, I release this prayer. Knowing that all my needs are met with ease and care."

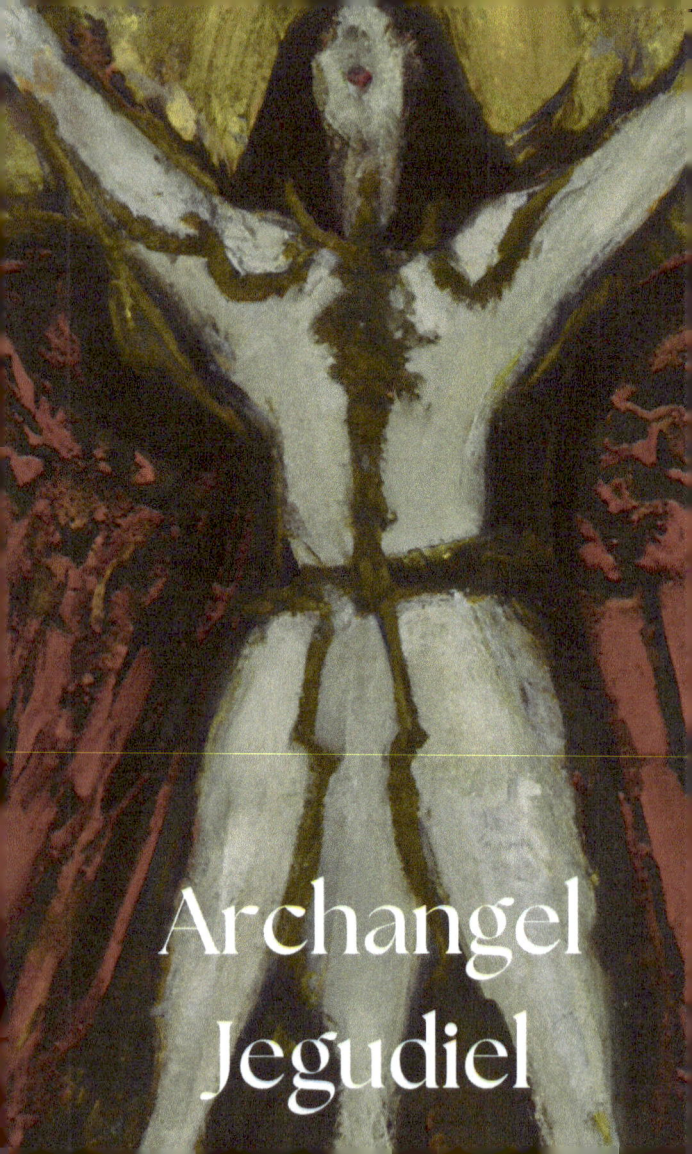

I am Jegudiel, angel of perseverance and strength. I come to remind you that no challenge is greater than the light that burns within you. Every obstacle you face is not a punishment, but an invitation - a chance to rise, to grow, and to discover the depth of your own resilience. When the path seems steep or uncertain, do not lose heart. Stand firm, breathe deeply, and take the next step. I am with you, steadying your spirit and guiding you toward triumph.

I encourage you to trust the wisdom of your own intuition, for your inner voice knows the way. Listen to the quiet stirrings of your heart, and follow them with courage. As you align with your true purpose, your life will blossom with meaning and fulfillment.

Above all, remember gratitude. By honoring the blessings you already hold, you open yourself to even greater abundance and joy.

Archangel Jegudiel Mantra...

"I call upon Archangel Jegudiel to strengthen my spirit. I walk with courage, trust my inner guidance, and give thanks for the blessings that fill my life."

I am Zaphkiel, angel of compassion and spiritual awakening, and I come to walk beside you on your sacred journey of growth. You may feel at times that you are alone, but you are never abandoned - the divine realm surrounds you, holding you in love and guiding each step forward.

I remind you to trust the process of healing and transformation, even when it stirs discomfort or brings old wounds to the surface. Growth is rarely effortless, but it is always purposeful. Every challenge you face, every lesson you learn, is shaping you into the fullest expression of your soul.

I encourage you to make space for your spirit each day. Through prayer, meditation, stillness, or quiet reflection, you open a channel to the divine and invite wisdom to flow through you. Trust this unfolding. Embrace your transformation, and know that I am here, guiding you into the light of your awakening.

Archangel Zaphkiel Mantra...

"I call upon Archangel Zaphkiel to guide my heart toward healing and awakening. I trust the process of transformation and open myself to the wisdom of the divine."

I am Cassiel, guardian of patience and quiet perseverance. I come to remind you that all things unfold in their perfect season. The delays, the pauses, the waiting - they are not punishments but part of a greater rhythm that leads you exactly where you are meant to be. Trust the timing of your life. Even when the way forward feels hidden, the universe is arranging each step with care.

I call you to release the need for instant answers and instead walk steadily, with faith. Growth takes time. Healing takes time. Dreams take time. Be patient with yourself as you learn, stumble, and rise again. Every challenge you face is an invitation to grow stronger, wiser, and more resilient.

Do not lose heart when progress feels slow. Each small step you take is a victory. Trust your path, and know that I walk beside you always.

Archangel Cassiel Mantra...

"I call upon Archangel Cassiel to bless me with patience and strengthen my perseverance. I trust divine timing and walk forward with steady faith."

I am Metatron, guardian of divine energy and wisdom, and I come to remind you of who you truly are. You are not small, not limited, not forgotten - you are a radiant being of light, created with infinite potential. The power to shape your world and co create your reality flows through you in every breath, in every thought, in every choice you make.

Pause now and connect with your inner wisdom. Feel the quiet pulse of the universe moving through you, guiding you toward the path that has always been yours. Trust that you stand exactly where you are meant to stand, that every step is part of divine timing, unfolding with perfect precision even when you cannot see the full picture. Trust yourself.

Archangel Metatron Mantra...

"Divine Metatron, please guide me to align with my highest path and purpose. Help me to connect with my inner wisdom and intuition, and to trust in the universe's plan for me. Please infuse me with the wisdom and knowledge I need to navigate this journey with grace and ease."

I am Zacharial, angel of healing, forgiveness, and compassion. I come to remind you that true healing begins with love - the love you offer yourself and the love you extend to others. If you are holding onto anger, grief, or resentment, know that these burdens are not yours to carry forever. Release them now, and let forgiveness be the key that unlocks your freedom.

I invite you to care for yourself as tenderly as the Divine cares for you. Nurture your body with rest, your mind with peace, and your heart with kindness. Establish boundaries that honor your energy, for you are worthy of balance and wholeness.

And as you heal, let your compassion flow outward. A kind word, a gentle touch, a moment of understanding - these small acts ripple into the world and return to you as blessings. Trust that I walk beside you, guiding you into peace.

Archangel Zacherial Mantra...

"I call upon Archangel Zacharial to fill me with healing light. I release resentment, embrace forgiveness, and open my heart to love and compassion."

I am Ariel, guardian of nature and the flow of abundance. I call you back to the rhythm of the Earth, for within her beauty you will rediscover your own. The trees, the rivers, the wind, the creatures great and small - all are teachers, all are reminders of the balance that sustains life. When you pause to honor and protect the natural world, you align yourself with its harmony, and in that harmony, blessings multiply.

I remind you that abundance is not something you must chase - it is your divine birthright. Open your heart to receive prosperity in every form: love, joy, peace, and the resources you need to flourish. When you choose balance, when you give and receive in equal measure, the universe responds by pouring more light into your life.

Walk gently, honor the Earth, and trust that as you care for creation, creation cares for you.

Archangel Ariel Mantra...

"I call upon Archangel Ariel to guide me into harmony with nature. I honor the Earth, embrace balance, and open my heart to divine abundance."

I am Zephaniel, angel of creativity and sacred expression. I come to awaken the gifts that live within you, the ones you were born to share with the world. You carry within your soul a unique light, a song, a vision that no one else can bring forth in the same way. Do not allow fear, doubt, or the weight of comparison to silence your spirit. You were created to express, to create, to inspire.

Take time to nurture yourself and your artistry. In the quiet spaces, you will hear the whispers of inspiration and feel the flow of divine energy guiding your hands, your voice, your heart. Trust what stirs within you, for it is a sacred seed placed by the Creator.

Share your gifts boldly. Each word, each brushstroke, each note you release is a blessing to the world. Shine without hesitation, for your light is needed.

Archangel Zephaniel Mantra...

"I call upon Archangel Zephaniel to awaken my creative spirit. I trust my unique voice, I release all fear, and I shine my light with joy and confidence."

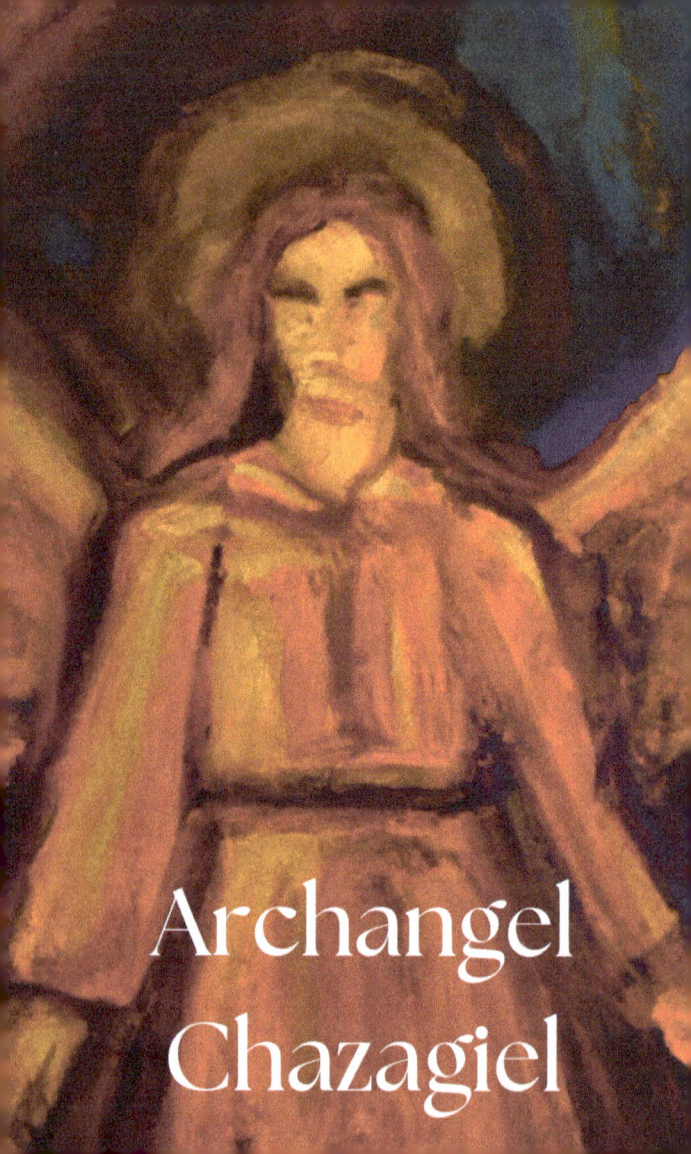

I am Chazagiel, the angel of creativity and divine inspiration. I come to remind you that within you lives a wellspring of unique gifts, talents, and visions that no one else can bring into the world. You are an artist of life, and your soul longs to express itself in ways that are fresh, authentic, and true. Do not silence your ideas or dismiss them as unworthy - they are sparks of divine light meant to shine through you.

Inspiration often arrives quietly, in places you least expect: a whisper in nature, a melody in your heart, a sudden thought that feels alive with possibility. Open yourself to receive these gifts.

Remember also to nourish your spirit. Rest when you need to, create when you feel called, and give yourself permission to find joy in the process. As you honor your creativity, you awaken the beauty of your soul.

Archangel Chazagiel Mantra...

"I call upon Archangel Chazagiel to awaken my creativity and guide my imagination. I welcome new ideas with joy, and I honor the divine spark within me."

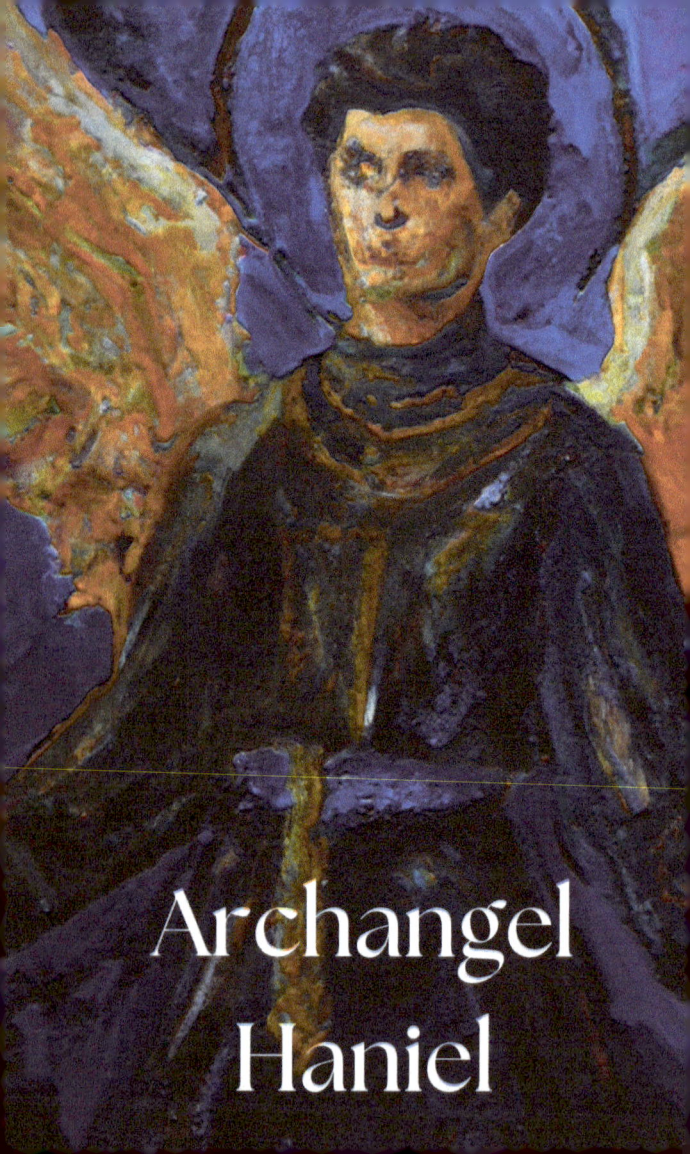

I am Haniel, angel of intuition, balance, and grace. I whisper to you in the quiet moments, in the stillness of your heart, guiding you gently toward truth. Trust what you feel, even if others do not understand it, for your inner wisdom is a sacred gift from the Divine.

I call you to walk in balance. Let your spirit find harmony between giving and receiving, work and rest, strength and softness. When you align with balance, peace flows into every corner of your life, grounding you and lifting you at the same time.

I also remind you of the power of grace and forgiveness. Release the weight of resentment, forgive yourself for past mistakes, and extend compassion to those who have caused you pain. In doing so, you free your heart and make space for joy. Trust yourself, beloved one, and let love guide every step

Archangel Haniel Mantra...

"I call upon Archangel Haniel to awaken my intuition and restore my balance. With grace and compassion, I release what weighs me down and walk in the wisdom of love."

I am Zathael, angel of transformation and divine growth. I come to remind you that change is not something to fear, but a sacred doorway into the fullness of who you are becoming. Every season of your life carries purpose, even when it feels uncertain or unfamiliar. Trust that what falls away now makes space for what is ready to bloom within you.

Listen to the quiet voice of your soul, for it is through your intuition that the Divine guides your every step. You are being led toward the path that was written for you long before you could see it. When doubts rise or old patterns try to hold you back, release them into my care.

Step boldly into your own power. Embrace the journey of becoming, for your true potential is vast and radiant. I walk beside you, reminding you that you are safe, guided, and free.

Archangel Zathael Mantra...

"I call upon Archangel Zathael to guide my transformation. I release all that holds me back, trust my inner wisdom, and embrace the fullness of who I am becoming."

I am Cornucopia, angel of divine abundance and sacred prosperity. I come to remind you that abundance is not reserved for a chosen few - it is the birthright of every soul, including you. Release the belief that you are lacking or unworthy. Open your heart to see the blessings that already surround you, for gratitude unlocks the flow of even greater gifts.

Abundance is not measured only in wealth or possessions. It is found in love shared, laughter that lifts your spirit, the beauty of the earth, and the relationships that nourish your soul. When you celebrate these treasures, you align with the natural flow of prosperity.

Do not be afraid to receive. The universe longs to fill your life with goodness, peace, and joy. Trust that what is meant for you will always find you. I am with you, guiding you into a life of overflowing grace.

Archangel Cornucopia Mantra...

"I call upon Archangel Cornucopia to open the flow of abundance in my life. I am worthy of love, joy, and prosperity, and I welcome every blessing with gratitude."

I am Barachiel, bearer of blessings and angel of joy. I come to remind you that your life is already overflowing with gifts, even in moments when you may not see them. Each sunrise, each breath, each smile shared with another is evidence of the Divine's love for you. When you pause to notice these blessings and give thanks, your heart expands, and gratitude becomes a light that shines through everything you do.

I encourage you to live with kindness, to let your words and actions be blessings to those around you. A simple smile, a gentle gesture, or a compassionate thought can ripple outward farther than you can imagine. As you lift others, you also rise, and joy flows back to you multiplied.

Celebrate the present moment, for it is sacred. Trust that you are cherished, supported, and surrounded by endless love.

Archangel Barachiel Mantra...

"I call upon Archangel Barachiel to open my heart to joy. I am grateful for the blessings in my life, and I share kindness and love with the world."

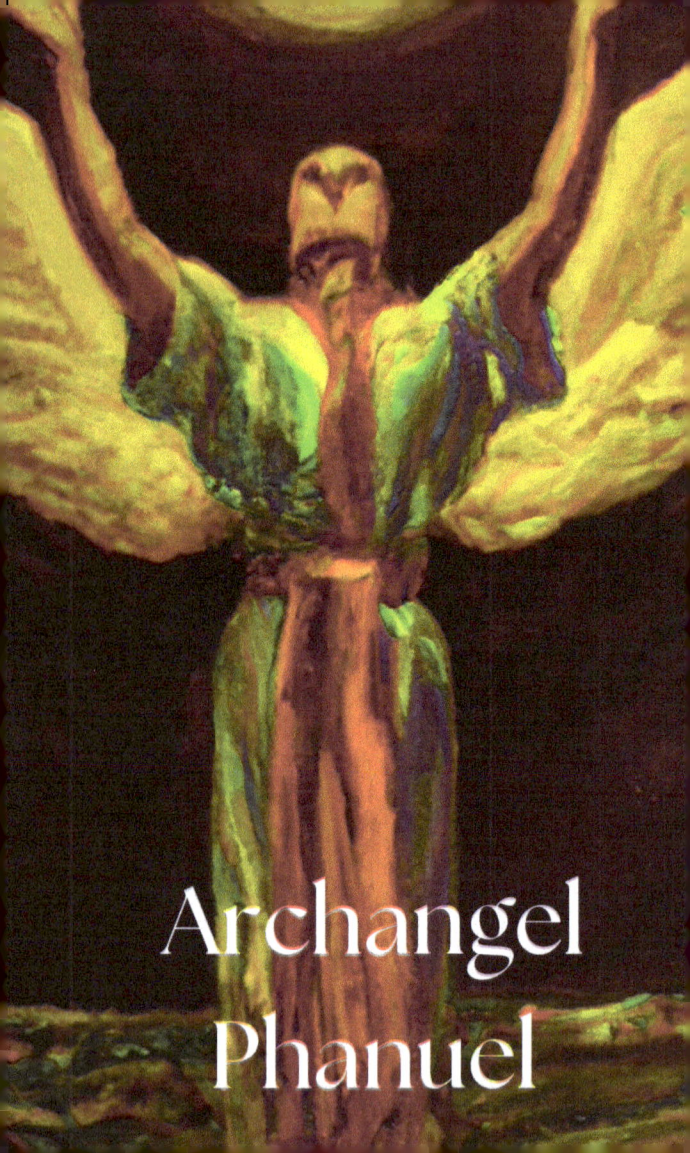

I am Phanuel, bearer of divine hope and renewal. I come to remind you that no darkness is permanent, no night is endless. The light of the Divine shines upon you now, illuminating the path ahead, even when you feel lost or uncertain. Trust that every step, even the ones that feel heavy, is guiding you toward your highest good.

You are deeply loved and constantly supported, even in moments when you cannot feel it. Your angels surround you, offering strength, comfort, and guidance with every breath you take. Release the fears, doubts, and old burdens you have carried for too long. They do not define you.

I encourage you to lift your gaze toward the horizon of what is possible. You are a powerful co creator of your destiny. With faith in yourself and trust in the universe, you can call forth joy, love, and endless renewal.

Archangel Phanuel Mantra...

"I call upon Archangel Phanuel to fill my spirit with hope and renewal. I release fear, embrace divine light, and trust the path unfolding before me."

I am Asariel, angel of vision and divine clarity. I come to lift the veil from your eyes so you may see the truth that has always lived within you. Your inner wisdom is a compass, guiding you through confusion and doubt. Trust the quiet whispers of your intuition - they are the language of your soul and the voice of the Divine speaking directly to your heart.

I encourage you to honor the power of vision. When you set intentions with love and clarity, you call your dreams into being. See yourself already living the life you long for, and feel the joy of it filling every corner of your spirit.

Do not be afraid of what you cannot yet see. Clarity comes step by step, as you walk forward in trust. I walk with you, shining light on your path, reminding you of your inner wisdom and strength.

Archangel Asariel Mantra...

"I call upon Archangel Asariel to open my inner vision. I trust my intuition, set clear intentions, and walk with clarity toward my highest good."

I am Uriel, the light of God, and I come to awaken you to truth and understanding. My radiance shines into the places where confusion and doubt have hidden your clarity. In every challenge, there is wisdom waiting to be revealed. Trust that I can illuminate what feels uncertain, so you may see clearly and step forward with confidence.

I invite you to open your heart and mind to the divine guidance flowing toward you. Let go of the shadows of fear, guilt, or old patterns that no longer serve your growth. When you release them into my care, peace and forgiveness will gently fill the space they leave behind.

Remember, beloved one, you are never without light. The spark of the Divine burns within you, steady and eternal. Trust this light, follow its glow, and you will always find the path to truth, healing, and inner harmony.

Archangel Uriel Mantra...

"I call upon Archangel Uriel to fill me with divine light and clarity. I release fear, embrace truth, and walk forward with peace and understanding."

I am Zuriel, angel of strength, courage, and perseverance. I see the challenges that rise before you, the obstacles that seem immovable, and I remind you: within your heart lies a power greater than any barrier. You are not fragile - you are resilient, capable, and stronger than you believe.

When fear whispers that you are not enough, I encourage you to step forward anyway. Courage is not the absence of fear; it is the choice to keep moving despite it. Each bold step you take calls forth new opportunities and opens doors that once seemed sealed.

I urge you to persevere. When the path feels steep or uncertain, know that you are not walking it alone. The divine realm surrounds you, supporting you, strengthening you, guiding you. Trust the journey, beloved one. Hold to your vision, keep your heart open, and you will reach the success your soul seeks.

Archangel Zuriel Mantra...

"I call upon Archangel Zuriel to fill me with strength, courage, and perseverance. I move forward with faith, trusting the universe to guide me to my highest good."

The Answers You Seek

Are Within

More from Amanda Clarke
The Literary Oracle
www.theliteracyoracle.com

The "Daily Guidance" series offers an innovative approach to finding spiritual wisdom and practical advice. Each book in the series is a unique tool designed for daily introspection and decision-making. Readers are invited to meditate on a question or seek general guidance for the day, then flip to a random page in the book. The page they land on provides a personalized message from various spiritual sources, such as angels, tarot, or spirit animals. With each turn of the page, these books deliver insightful, positive messages and mantras to inspire personal growth and provide clarity on life's daily challenges and decisions.

Other books in this series:-
The Angelic Oracles
Daily Angel Tarot Reading
Mystic Tarot Cat
Oracle of the Tarot Cat
Vibes Unveiled
Spirit Animal Oracle
Answers from the Oracles
Messages from the Angels

 Support Indie Magic

Love your daily guidance? You can grab more of my books direct from The Literary Oracle:
www.theliteraryoracle.com

Buying direct means:
- Better prices for you
- More support for me as an indie author
- More magical books in your hands

My books are also available worldwide through online bookstores, but direct purchases help keep the magic flowing.

Thank you for supporting indie creativity! ⭐

Scan me

More on the Bookshelves at www.theliteraryoracle.com

www.ingramcontent.com/pod-product-compliance
Lightning Source LLC
Chambersburg PA
CBHW061730070526
44583CB00024B/3087